Celebrity Biographies

Taylor Lautner

FILM SUPERSTAR

ALLY AZZARELLI

Enslow Publishers, Inc.
40 Industrial Road
Box 398
Berkeley Heights, NJ 07922
USA
http://www.enslow.com

For Amanda Johnson

Library of Congress Cataloging-in-Publication Data:

Azzarelli, Ally.
    Taylor Lautner : film superstar / by Ally Azzarelli.
        p. cm. — (Hot celebrity biographies)
    Includes index.
    Summary: "Read about Taylor's early life in Michigan, how he got into acting, and his involvement in the Twilight
        series"—Provided by publisher.
    ISBN 978-0-7660-3874-5
    1. Lautner, Taylor, 1992—Juvenile literature. 2. Actors—United States—Biography—Juvenile literature.
    I. Title. II. Series.
    PN2287.L2855A99 2011
    791.4302'8092—dc22
    [B]   2010048125

Paperback ISBN: 978-1-59845-288-4

Printed in the United States of America

052011 Lake Book Manufacturing, Inc., Melrose Park, IL

10 9 8 7 6 5 4 3 2 1

To Our Readers: We have done our best to make sure all Internet addresses in this book were active and appropriate when we went to press. However, the author and the publisher have no control over and assume no liability for the material available on those Internet sites or on other Web sites they may link to. Any comments or suggestions can be sent by e-mail to comments@enslow.com or to the address on the back cover.

♻ Enslow Publishers, Inc., is committed to printing our books on recycled paper. The paper in every book contains 10% to 30% post-consumer waste (PCW). The cover board on the outside of each book contains 100% PCW. Our goal is to do our part to help young people and the environment too!

Illustration Credits: AP Photo/Alberto Pellaschiar pp. 14, 18; AP Photo/Chris Pizzello, pp. 1, 22, 34; AP Photo/Chris Pizzello/FILE, p. 8; AP Photo/Damian Dovargenes, p. 28; AP Photo/Dennis Poroy, pp. 25, 30; AP Photo/Evan Agostini, p. 33; AP Photo/Katsumi Kasahara, p. 20; AP Photo/Luis Martinez, p. 12; AP Photo/Matt Sayles, pp. 4, 6, 16, 36, 38; AP Photo/PRNewsFoto/CVS/pharmacy, Jesse Grant, p. 41.

Cover Illustration: AP Photo/Chris Pizzello (Taylor Lautner at *The Twilight Saga: Eclipse* premiere.)

Contents

Meet Taylor Lautner!

There was once a time when Taylor Lautner was just a regular kid. He could hit the mall or go to a football game without anyone noticing. That was before he became Jacob Black in the *Twilight* saga.

Today, people park their cars outside his family's home and try to take his picture. Fans and paparazzi follow him around airports, shopping centers, and restaurants. Taylor never imagined the popularity he would have one day. He told *GQ* magazine about a scary time when he and his costar Kristen Stewart were swarmed by fans at a hotel in Brazil.

"We were in lockdown in this little room for forty-five minutes waiting for the SWAT team to arrive. We said to each other, 'Let's say they get into this room. What are they going to do? Tear us to shreds?'"

Yes, life sure has changed for this talented young actor. It's as if he were thrown into the spotlight almost overnight. Taylor went from playing the cute, young

◄ *The movie* Twilight *premiered on November 17, 2008, in Los Angeles. But Taylor Lautner was just getting a taste of the fame that was to come.*

TAYLOR TIDBITS

Full Name: Taylor Daniel Lautner

Birthday: February 11, 1992

Ethnicity: French, German, Dutch, and American Indian—his mom is part Potawatomi and Ottawa Indian

Birthplace: Grand Rapids, Michigan

Height: 5' 10"

Family: Mom, Deborah, and Dad, Daniel, and younger sister, Makena

First Jobs: Commercials, bit parts on TV including *My Wife and Kids* and *The Bernie Mac Show*

Secret: Taylor felt bullied in school. "I was never extremely confident," he told *Rolling Stone* magazine. "Because I was an actor, when I was in school there was a little bullying going on. Not physical bullying but people making fun of what I do."

overachiever Eliot Murtaugh in *Cheaper by the Dozen 2* to the dark and mysterious Jacob Black in *Twilight*. He has admitted acting wasn't even his first love. As a youngster growing up in Michigan, Taylor was all about martial arts and sports.

KARATE KID

Taylor Daniel Lautner's exciting journey began on February 11, 1992. That's the day his mom, Deborah, and dad, Dan, welcomed their firstborn into the world.

(Taylor's sister was born six years later.) When he was born, his mom was a project manager at Herman Miller, a trendy office furniture design firm, and his dad was a commercial airline pilot.

As a child, Taylor loved playing all types of sports. He enjoyed baseball, basketball, football, horseback riding, and karate. He began studying karate at the age of six. The first martial arts school he attended was Fabiano's Karate & Fitness Center in Holland, Michigan. After only a year, he was competing against other students. Even better, he won three first-place trophies. During one of his competitions, Taylor met a popular martial arts expert named Mike Chaturantabut, better known as Mike Chat.

Chat introduced Taylor to XMA (Extreme Martial Arts), a sport that combines karate kicks, gymnastics, and flips performed to upbeat music. Taylor worked hard to perfect his XMA moves. He practiced five or six days a week for two or three hours a day. It wasn't easy balancing friends, school, and other sports with XMA. But Taylor found that his hard work made all the difference.

Chat did more than just help perfect his moves. He encouraged Taylor to act. Chat had some experience working in Hollywood. He played the part of Chad Lee, the Blue Power Ranger on the *Power Rangers* TV series.

TAY'S FAVES

Movies: Action or adventure movies including *The Dark Knight*, *Braveheart*, and *Iron Man*

Music: U2, Britney Spears, and the Black Eyed Peas

Actors: Matt Damon, Brad Pitt, Denzel Washington, and Mark Wahlberg

Celebrity Crushes: Jessica Alba and Megan Fox

Team: University of Michigan Wolverines football

Foods: Chinese, Mexican, burgers, pizza, steaks, and ice cream

Ice Cream: Hudsonville Ice Cream's cake batter flavor

Cake: Red Velvet

Hobbies: Karate, running, watching football, bowling, and playing Wii

Color: Blue

Even though Taylor lived in Michigan, Chat encouraged him to try out for a Burger King commercial in California. However, the producers of the TV commercial were looking for an older actor. But Taylor enjoyed trying out for the part and refused to give up on acting.

FROM MICHIGAN TO CALIFORNIA

Taylor lived in the Grand Rapids, Michigan area until he was about eleven. While in Michigan, Taylor attended Jamestown Elementary School. It was around age ten that

Taylor began flying back and forth to California to take part in acting auditions for various TV and movie roles.

Taylor landed his first role in 2001, playing the part of young Kismet in the science fiction film *Shadow Fury*. The role gave him the chance to show off his martial arts skills. It also opened the door to more auditions. However, most of the auditions were in California.

"They'd call at 9 or 10 at night, which was 6 or 7 their time, and say, 'We've got an audition tomorrow—can you be here?' We'd leave really early in the morning and get there about noon," Taylor later told his hometown paper. "I'd go to the audition in the afternoon, take the red-eye [late-night flight] back to Grand Rapids then go to school."

With this in mind, his family moved to the Los Angeles area to help Taylor try out for movies and TV. Moving from one state to another is never easy. Leaving behind friends, teammates, and relatives can be very difficult. Taylor admits this big change wasn't easy, but in the end it was worth it. "It was a big deal to leave," Taylor told MLive.com. "All our family was there."

Knowing the move was a big decision, Taylor's family agreed to try California for one month. During the last few days of their temporary stay, Taylor got a callback

for a *Rugrats* commercial for Nickelodeon. The Lautner family gave California another six months, and from there, Taylor's acting jobs kept on coming!

While living in Santa Clarita, California, Taylor attended Rio Norte Junior High and Valencia High School. Because of his busy schedule, he left school in the tenth grade. He was able to take a special test that allowed him to complete high school early. Taylor began taking courses at a local community college while auditioning for TV and movies.

THE ROLES ROLL IN

From 2003 to 2004, Taylor landed several voice-over roles and guest spots on shows. Fans may recall seeing him on *The Bernie Mac Show*, *Summerland*, and *The Nick & Jessica Variety Hour*. Although he was getting lots of great experience, it wasn't until 2005 that a then thirteen-year-old Taylor scored big parts in two popular movies.

In June 2005, Taylor appeared as Sharkboy in *The Adventures of Sharkboy and Lavagirl in 3-D* by *Spy Kids* producer and director Robert Rodriguez. "We freaked out [when I got the role] my whole family couldn't sleep for, like, a week," confessed Taylor to his hometown paper, the *Grand Rapids Press*.

In the film, a ten-year-old lonely child named Max creates two imaginary best friends. One is the powerful Sharkboy and the other is fire-making Lavagirl (played by actress Taylor Dooley). Max is surprised to learn that his imaginary friends are actually real. They ask him to help take on the evil Mr. Electric (played by actor George Lopez).

"The minute I heard the words 'Sharkboy' and 'Lavagirl', I knew it was about superheroes and I was interested!" said Taylor. "[When] I read the script and I really liked Sharkboy, because he wasn't just a superhero but he had this really interesting life where he was searching for his long-lost father and I thought he was kind of funny and different. I liked that he was super athletic," he explained.

Right in time for Christmas of 2005, moviegoers caught Taylor as Eliot Murtaugh in *Cheaper by the Dozen 2* alongside Hillary Duff, Steve Martin, and real-life friend, Alyson Stoner. Mayhem breaks out when the oversized Baker family encounters the rich and successful Murtaughs. Although the kids get along, their dads are supercompetitive rivals.

Taylor played the adorable preteen son, Eliot, whom tomboyish Sarah Baker (played by Alyson Stoner) develops a crush on. "Working with Alyson was

▲ *Taylor Lautner was only thirteen when he attended the premiere of* The Adventures of Sharkboy and Lavagirl in 3-D *in Hollywood.*

wonderful. We played Ping-Pong. We had Karaoke night, we enjoyed waterskiing, it was a lot of fun," Taylor said in a video they made for Alyson's YouTube page.

It was during the making of *Cheaper by the Dozen 2* that Taylor developed a new outlook on moviemaking. "That's when I stopped looking at movie stars as movie stars, and just looked at them as people," he told the *Grand Rapids Press*. Being on the set with well-known actors and moviemakers surely helped prepare Taylor for bigger roles. Upon filming both movies, Taylor met with reporters and learned the ins and outs of promoting his new films.

The Adventures of Sharkboy and Lavagirl in 3-D and *Cheaper by the Dozen 2* introduced fans to Taylor. Teen mags began featuring photos and stories on the young actor. It was only a matter of time before he became a star. Taylor once joked that even moms began recognizing him as Sharkboy.

As if Taylor could tell the future, after filming *The Adventures of Sharkboy and Lavagirl in 3-D* and *Cheaper by the Dozen 2*, he told *Access Hollywood*, "I think I need a drama ... something really serious." Little did he know his wish was about to come true.

Twilight Time

In 2008, Taylor played Jack Spivey, the son of Christian Slater's character, Henry, on the short-lived NBC series *My Own Worst Enemy*. While working on the series, Taylor auditioned for the hunky werewolf in a movie adaptation of Stephenie Meyer's book series *Twilight*. On February 7, 2008, an MTV blog said that the *Twilight* directors had yet to cast the role of Jacob. Fans were posting messages online, guessing who would win the role of the werewolf. Everyone was anxious to hear just who would play Jacob.

A month after the audition, Taylor got a call saying they narrowed the part down to three actors, including him! After hearing that, he decided to go online and search for *Twilight* information and was surprised to see that everyone was talking about the movie. The pressure was on! "I thought, 'Oh my goodness. If I get this, it'll be huge.' I realized I really want this," Taylor told the *Grand Rapids Press*.

◄ *Taylor poses with a movie poster depicting him as the character Jacob Black.*

Twilight Cheat Sheet

What is *Twilight*?: *Twilight* is the first of a series of fantasy/romance movies based upon four books by Stephenie Meyer. The first film introduces the main characters and centers around a budding relationship between Bella Swan (Kristen Stewart) and handsome vampire Edward Cullen (Robert Pattinson). Because the Cullen family is not like other vampires, Edward and his family try to protect Bella from a group of dangerous bloodsuckers. Taylor Lautner's character, Jacob, is a loyal friend to Bella.

What about the sequels?: In *New Moon*, Jacob, who is actually a werewolf, and Bella become very close as he tries to protect her from Victoria, a vampire who wants to kill Bella. In *Eclipse*, there are new battles to fight, and Jacob professes his love for Bella, who plans to marry Edward. In *Breaking Dawn*, Bella and Edward are expecting their first child.

Who else is in the *Twilight* saga?: The series of films also features Dakota Fanning, Peter Facinelli, and Ashley Greene, who have become big stars as well.

▷ Stephenie Meyer is the author of the Twilight *series.*

Taylor was obviously overjoyed to win the part of the werewolf Jacob Black. Unfamiliar with the *Twilight* books, Taylor knew it was important for him to learn more about his character and the story line. "Before I was cast I hadn't even heard of *Twilight*. So then when I was actually cast I did my research, and I was like, 'Oh, what am I getting myself into?'"

To better understand his role, he read the *Twilight* books. He told *Life Story* magazine he thinks Stephenie Meyer is such an amazing author. He explained that her detailed writing really helped him understand Jacob, the teenage son of Billy Black, an elder of the Quileute Indians.

Taylor also wanted to learn more about the Quileute people. While researching, he actually found out more about his own nationality. An American Indian in real life, Taylor is Potawatomi and Ottawa Indian on his mom's side.

Taylor got to interview Quileute teens. He was surprised to learn they had a lot in common with him! They all had strong family values and loved sports and the beach. "We went out to dinner with them and got a chance to talk to them . . . they're just like me. They showed up in basketball uniforms."

Who is Jacob Black?

His Nickname: Jake
Species: Werewolf
Parents: Billy Black, mom Sarah Black has passed away
Siblings: Older twin sisters, Rachel and Rebecca

Taylor Lautner's Description of Jacob: "He's a family friend of the Swans, Bella's family. He's really fun and outgoing, easy to talk to and easy to relate to . . . I'm pretty similar to that side of him. And, he's got a pretty big crush on Bella."

Author, Stephenie Meyer's Description of Jacob: "Jacob was my first experience with a character taking over—a minor character developing such roundness and life that I couldn't keep him locked inside a tiny role . . . From the very beginning, even when Jacob only appeared in chapter six of *Twilight*, he was so alive. I liked him. More than I should for such a small part."

▲ Above is a movie-poster version of Taylor Lautner as Jacob Black.

TAYLOR'S TWILIGHT EXPERIENCE

Once filming began, Taylor really connected with his costars. Even though, at sixteen, he was the youngest on the set at the time, Taylor had a blast with the other actors. His only minor complaint was that he had to wear an itchy wig of long hair. "The most difficult part for me was the wig. It took a while to put on and take off." Other than that, he really took to playing the role.

Acting is a job, and at any job, it is very important to get along with your coworkers. In Taylor's case his costars are his coworkers. The cast and crew spend days and weeks working closely together. Being able to work well together is a must. According to Taylor, this wasn't a problem for him and cast members Robert Pattinson and Kristen Stewart. In fact, he considers them his good friends. "The great thing about this series is how the whole cast is so close. It would be a nightmare if we weren't. It would be impossible to make this series because the characters are so tight. We're really thankful that we all get along so well."

The actors have great chemistry off the set. In behind-the-scenes interviews and YouTube blooper footage, the cast members are usually joking with each other. Kristen and Robert play fight and lovingly tease Taylor. In TV interviews they laugh and discuss heated moments such as the famous *Eclipse* tent scene.

▲ *The stars of the* Twilight *movies get along really well. Above, Taylor Lautner (left), Kristen Stewart, and Robert Pattinson (right) share a laugh while promoting* Twilight *in Japan.*

20

"The most challenging thing was having to hate Edward, because Rob plays Edward," Taylor said in an I Heart Radio interview. "We get along so well and are such good friends. Sometimes we couldn't keep a straight face." Taylor and Rob joke about intense scenes where they tried hard not to burst out laughing. In the movie, their characters are fighting for Bella's love, but in real life, the actors are all good friends.

The cast members refer to themselves as "one big family." After a long day of shooting, they would sit down for group dinners or hang out in each other's trailers. Kristen and Rob love playing guitar. They would sometimes jam offset, entertaining the cast.

Between the fans and the press, the *Twilight* stars are under a lot of pressure. Having good relationships with each other is important. Taylor, Robert, and Kristen joke about the fans supporting Team Jacob and Team Edward. They all adore their fans and don't compete for the spotlight. This helps them maintain a very special friendship.

Taylor's Transformation

A month after *Twilight* hit the theaters, rumors spread about who would play Jacob in the next movie, *The Twlight Saga: New Moon*. *Entertainment Weekly* magazine reported that the movie studio was looking to replace Taylor in the sequel. In the story, the character Jacob has grown older. The producers wanted to cast a more muscular actor to fit the part. Gossip began to buzz about two actors who might steal the role from Taylor.

Scorpion King 2 actor Michael Copon and *The Chronicles of Narnia: Prince Caspian* star Ben Barnes were said to be perfect for the part. Michael Copon even announced it on his personal Facebook page!

Fans were not happy about the idea of another actor playing Jacob. Because of his fans' Web site petitions and protests, Taylor knew he had to build muscle. Not just to get the role for himself, but also for his fans. He wouldn't want to let them down. He couldn't lose the part he was

◄ *Taylor gained muscle for the movie* The Twilight Saga: New Moon. *This photo was taken when he won a Scream award on October 17, 2009, for his work in the film.*

meant to play! "I've been working out since the day we stopped filming *Twilight*," Taylor told MTV, "I'm gonna be ready if my number's called."

The young actor worked out vigorously with a gym trainer and doubled the amount of food he normally ate. Taylor ate every two hours. He even went as far as carrying beef patties around with him and supersizing his portions. "At one point, my trainer said, 'Put anything in your mouth. Go to McDonald's, get the biggest shake possible. I just need to get calories in you,'" said Taylor.

Good News!
Fans surely were relieved to read the following post from *New Moon* director Chris Weitz on Stephenie Meyer's Web site, "I'm very happy to announce that Taylor Lautner will be playing Jacob Black in *New Moon* and that he's doing so with the enthusiastic support of Summit Entertainment, the producers, and Stephenie Meyer."

Taylor was thrilled to hear the news. When *E!* Online spoke to Taylor shortly after the announcement, he said, "I'm very excited. *Twilight* was an incredible experience and I'm just stoked to be back and work with the whole team again . . . I'm very excited to work with Chris Weitz, he's an extremely talented director so it's going to be great ."

Taylor went on to tell MTV, "My job for *Twilight* was to bring *Twilight* Jacob to life—the friendly, happy-go-lucky little Jacob. My job for *New Moon* is completely different. I've been looking forward to that."

There was plenty of action and adventure in store for Taylor. For example, while on the set of *New Moon*, Taylor got to do all of the dirt bike scenes himself. No need for a stunt double. Dirt bike riding was new for Taylor. "I had to do some practice in rehearsals so it looked like I could actually ride one. That was a lot of fun," he told *Life Story* magazine.

▼ Kristen Stewart, Taylor Lautner (middle), and Robert Pattinson have a good time as they answer questions about The Twilight Saga: New Moon at the Comic-Con International convention in San Diego.

Another standout moment for Taylor was the big werewolf transformation. In *New Moon*, Bella first finds out Jacob is a wolf and it is a very emotional scene. That's when Jacob realizes he may not be the best friend possible for Bella because of what he himself is going through.

A BREAK FROM *TWILIGHT*

Between the second and third *Twilight* films, Taylor's fans were treated to an extra special appearance. Taylor was able to show off his comedic talents by hosting *Saturday Night Live* on December 12, 2009. He started off his *SNL* guest-hosting duties with a very cool intro monologue. He joked about what he wished he'd done during rapper Kanye West's infamous interruption of singer Taylor Swift's acceptance speech at the 2009 MTV VMA Awards. Taylor had the live audience laughing out loud while karate kicking a cardboard cutout of Kanye. He then acted lovey-dovey to a cardboard version of Taylor Swift.

ON TO *ECLIPSE*

Taylor fans had to wait until the end of June 2010 to catch their favorite actor in the third *Twilight* film, *Eclipse*. "Jacob's matured a lot, so that was interesting," Taylor told MTV. "He becomes frustrated in this one and I can see why. He gets this close to the girl, and he's been fighting for her for a long time. He's extremely persistent

and he gets this close and then slammed down to the ground again and told, 'No.'" Taylor feels bad for his character adding, "I definitely would not want to be in Jacob's position."

When asked what was different between *Eclipse* and *New Moon*, Taylor said, "There was a lot more action in this picture, but for me, specifically, I am a wolf when there is any action going on. So, I was bummed that [because special effects were used for the wolf] I wasn't involved . . . too much. I got to kiss Bella for the first time. Yeah, so that was probably the biggest thing. That was probably the most exciting new thing." He joked about comparing notes with costar Robert on Kristen's kissing abilities.

MOVING ON TO *BREAKING DAWN*

Taylor joins his costars in the last two *Twilight* saga films *Breaking Dawn—Part 1* and *Breaking Dawn—Part 2*. The book is over five hundred pages, so the filmmakers wanted to break the story into two films. Anxious moviegoers weren't too happy to hear that they would have to wait another year between the two movies to see their favorite actors on the big screen again.

Those who like Taylor Lautner and his character Jacob Black are called Team Jacob and, on or off the screen, they can't get enough of their favorite breakout star.

Team Jacob

Taylor Lautner has an incredible amount of fans. Girls from Boston to Brazil are proud members of Team Jacob. "The competition that goes on between the Team Jacob fans and the Team Edward fans is my favorite part," Taylor told EW.com. When asked which team he himself would be on, he replied "Team Jacob of course!" Taylor told David Letterman about the different ways fans react to him in various countries. For example, he reports:

> In Japan, they're very sensitive—they cry a lot … they start crying, so you feel bad, and so you'll touch them or something and say 'It's OK, it's OK,"… and then they start crying more. So then you grab them with two hands or grab their shoulder and say "Seriously, it's going to be just fine," and they'll start bawling. And, eventually, they just faint. And, problem solved.

He went on to say, "In Brazil, they're very aggressive and physical . . . They literally would grab our legs and our arms . . . Then at the hotel . . . our security guard rushed

◀ *Fifteen-year-old* Twilight *fan Chloe Bates hugs a cardboard cutout of Taylor Lautner in her room.*

▲ Kristen Stewart says her friend Taylor Lautner will make a good husband for someone someday.

in, and closed the door and [told us to] remain calm . . . [they said] we got 2,000 girls that just stormed the lobby and got past hotel security and right now we're calling the Brazilian National Guard."

CELEBRITIES JOIN TEAM JACOB

Celebrities are also proud members of Team Jacob and support Taylor in the *Twilight* movies. *Day After Tomorrow* and *Phantom of the Opera* actress Emmy Rossum was seen carrying a Team Jacob water bottle getting out of a taxi at Los Angeles International Airport. TV star Kim Kardashian was also spotted carrying a Team Jacob water bottle around LA. MTV reality stars Lo Bosworth (*The Hills*) and Whitney Port (*The City*) both told PopSugar.com they're on Team Jacob.

Taylor's *Valentine's Day* costar Emma Roberts actually ran into some drama when she talked about Jacob on an episode of *The Tonight Show with Jay Leno*. Emma happened to be a guest alongside Robert Pattinson. When Jay asked which team she was on, she turned to Robert and replied, "I'm sorry, your hair looks wonderful in person, but I'm going to have to say Team Jacob." Reports say Emma received lots of angry tweets after that incident, which caused her to delete her Twitter account.

Surprisingly Taylor's close friend and onscreen crush, Kristen Stewart, seemed a bit torn about which guy would make a better husband. She told *Access Hollywood*, "I'm sure they would both be great husbands. Taylor is like one of the most steady [people]—he's really just a good guy. And then ... Rob is really a more, sort of analytical, thoughtful, like wishy-washy intellectual so it depends."

DATING RUMORS

Like most popular male celebrities, the rumors run wild whenever Taylor steps out with a girl. In February 2009, *J-14* magazine reported that Taylor admitted having a crush on singer/actress Selena Gomez in a radio interview. Selena described him as "awesome" and "amazing" on Ryan Seacrest's KIIS FM radio show, but said they are not a couple. In April 2009, *People* magazine claimed they had dinner in the Vancouver area while on a break from working on their movies. Ryan Seacrest confronted Taylor about Selena, and although Taylor admitted Selena was cute, he insisted they're just friends.

In the late fall of 2009 Taylor and his *Valentine's Day* costar Taylor Swift were said to be dating. Between Taylor Lautner's December 2009 *SNL* monologue, which referenced Swift, and their *Valentine's Day* onscreen kiss, the gossip magazines insisted the two were a couple.

The two denied they were an item even after the paparazzi caught them cruising around town in a sports car and at a Los Angeles Kings hockey game together. Taylor Swift told Country Music Radio, "He's an amazing guy and we're really close." At a *New Moon* press conference, Taylor Lautner was asked about Ms. Swift to which he replied, "The very funny thing is that all of you have seen every single move I make, so I guess I can leave that up to you to decide."

▼ Taylor Swift performs at the Z100 Jingle Ball in New York on December 11, 2009, right around the time that her rumored relationship with Taylor Lautner supposedly ended.

Within a few weeks, photos surfaced of Taylor having lunch at an Olive Garden restaurant with his high school sweetheart Sara Hicks, which of course led to talk of him cheating on Taylor Swift. However, it may have been Swift who broke his heart. In the fall of 2010, she released a song called "Back to December." She said this song was an apology to someone she hurt in a relationship. Some people think that the song was written for Taylor Lautner.

By March 2010, Taylor was rumored to be dating Emma Roberts. Celebrity blogs featured photos and captions stating that they became close after working on *Valentine's Day* together. *OK!* magazine talked to

Taylor Talks Girls

On Dating at 13: In 2005, at the premiere of *Cheaper by the Dozen 2* Taylor told reporters, "My dad says I can't date 'til I'm 28 but I'll have to negotiate that one down a little."

On Dating at 17: "I'm not dating one [girl]. I'm a teenager, I date," Taylor told Tyra on the *Tyra Banks Show*.

Perfect Girl: "Qualities I look for in a girl are loyalty, honesty and somebody who can totally let loose and be themselves and have fun."

Girlfriend Turnoffs: "If a girl doesn't know how to smile or laugh or if they try to play cool all the time. Playing hard to get is not the way to win me over. I'm definitely more for the girl who can smile and laugh all the time and just have a good time!"

First Kiss: "I think it was just with a random girl from school. I mean, it's not like I walked up to her and was like 'You're just a random girl and I'm going to kiss you,' but just a girl from school, and we had a little thing in junior high."

On Working With *Abduction* Costar and Rumored Girlfriend, Lily Collins: "She's extremely talented. Whenever [my character] Nathan crumbles, she has to always be there to support him. And she was."

On Dating a Fan: "I don't exclude anyone . . ."

▲ *A fan of Taylor Lautner takes her photo with him.*

a source close to Emma who said, "She thinks he's the cutest thing ever. They met on the set, and there was an instant attraction." Taylor and Emma were photographed together at the March 2010 *Vanity Fair* Oscar Party celebrating the 82nd Annual Academy Awards. A witness pointed out seeing Taylor put his arm around Emma at the party. Plus, people remembered Emma saying she was on Team Jacob when she was on *The Tonight Show*.

Fast-forward to summer of 2010, when the Internet began to buzz that Taylor was back with his high school sweetheart Sara Hicks. *Life & Style Weekly* magazine reported that an insider claimed the two "are definitely back on. She's absolutely gorgeous, and Taylor has always had a thing for her." Magazines also reported that she tweeted feeling sad to say good-bye around the same time that Taylor was on a trip out of town.

Starting in the fall of 2010, rumors surfaced that Taylor and his *Abduction* costar, Lily Collins, were becoming very close. As of spring 2011, they were said to still be boyfriend and girlfriend. Lily is the daughter of Phil Collins, a member of the band Genesis. Reports said that Taylor and Phil had met, and Dad approved!

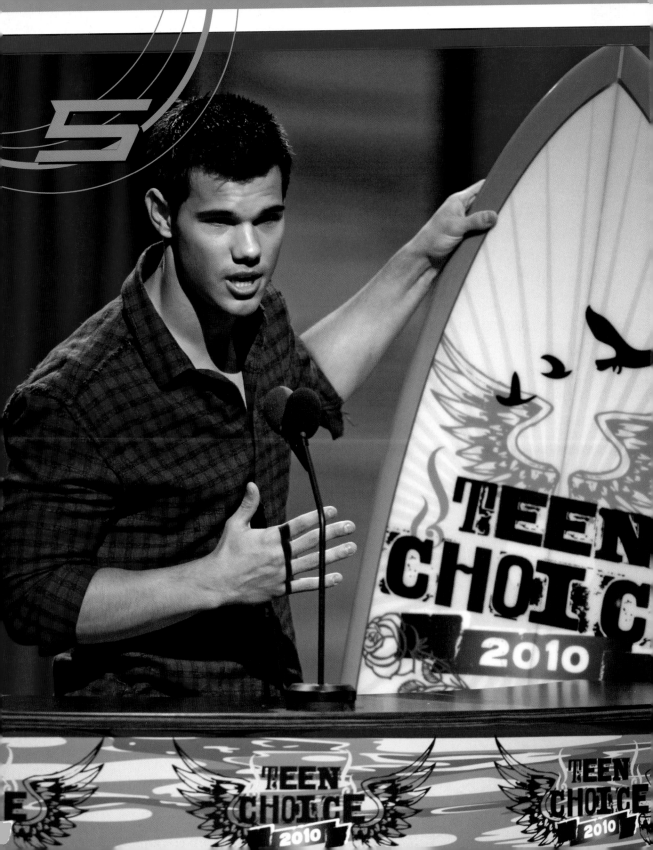

Staying Grounded

Even with lots of fans, fame, and fortune, Taylor Lautner stays focused and down to earth. "I'm the same person as before," Taylor told *Box Office* magazine. "It's just a completely different world. I have my world, and then I have *Twilight* world."

The *Grand Rapids Press* spoke to Taylor and his dad about his fame. Taylor promises that no matter how famous he gets, his parents simply won't let him get a big head because of it. "My parents wouldn't allow it. That's not the way they brought me up."

He may be a big star, but Taylor is a family guy at heart. Taylor is an awesome older brother to his sister, Makena. He even told *Seventeen* magazine that he is very protective of her. There are photos of them hanging out together on the set of his movies.

He is also close with his parents. He and his dad work out together, and his dad keeps a close eye on his career.

◄ *Taylor's star is going to keep rising. Here he accepts an award for Choice Smile at the Teen Choice Awards on August 10, 2010.*

Taylor knows that fans will approach him when he is out. It's a big part of being a popular actor. However, he tries to keep his personal life separate from his work. "When you go into this business, you film movies, go to events and fans recognize you . . . But when you go back to your regular world and you're with your family and friends, nothing has changed at all."

TAYLOR GIVES BACK

Another way Taylor keeps it real is by giving back to children in need. Taylor himself had a very scary life experience where he and his family needed help. At around age four, his home burned to the ground in an electrical fire. Luckily, Taylor and his mom were spending the night at his aunt's house because his father was away on business. "The police called and told us our house had burned down. If my aunt hadn't invited us to sleep over . . . well, wow." Taylor pointed out that his neighbors really stepped up and pitched in. "Everyone pulled together for us," he said of the donations of food and other items.

In the fall of 2008, Taylor auctioned himself off as part of a special Power of Youth online auction. The winning bidder enjoyed a one-hour lunch in Beverly Hills, California, with the teen star. Taylor helped raise $1,981 (the highest bidder), and the proceeds went to St. Jude Children's Research Hospital.

On the check:

CVS/pharmacy

PAY TO THE ORDER OF **Lollipop** THEATER NETWORK and [Best Buddies]

January 10, 2009   0109
DATE

One Hundred Thousand and 0/100

$ 100,000.⁰⁰

DOLLARS

MEMO access hollywood Stuff You Must Lounge

CVS/pharmacy

⑈0110200⑈:900981000⑈" 0109

▲ *Accepting a check from Rob Price (left) of CVS Pharmacy for the Best Buddies and Lollipop Theater Network charities are, from the right: actress Maureen McCormick, Access Hollywood host Billy Bush, Taylor Lautner, High School Musical star Vanessa Hudgens, and Nancy O'Dell of Access Hollywood.*

One of Taylor's favorite charities is the Lollipop Theater Network. Their mission is to entertain ill children who are confined to hospitals. The charity helps by bringing new movies into the hospital for the children and their families. In January 2009, he teamed up with *High School Musical* star Vanessa Hudgens and accepted a $100,000 check from CVS Pharmacy for the charity. In September

Contacting Taylor

Send all your fan mail to Taylor at this address:

Taylor Lautner
c/o Taylor Lautner Management
360 9111 Wilshire Blvd.
Beverly Hills, CA 90210

2010, Taylor won $40,000 in a lawsuit involving his trailer. He donated the entire winnings to the Lollipop Theater Network.

Taylor has also been a part of events such as the 2010 pre-Super Bowl DirecTV Celebrity Beach Bowl and generous online charity auctions. In April 2010, he personalized and auctioned off a messenger bag benefiting the Books for Kids Foundation. The Books for Kids Foundation donates books, creates libraries, and promotes reading.

A BRIGHT FUTURE

Thanks to a close-knit family and incredible discipline, Taylor is focused on his future, his career, and continued success. In 2009, Taylor's dad, Dan Lautner, formed a production company called Tailor Made Entertainment. The action film *Cancun* is the first movie planned by Tailor Made Entertainment. Although as of spring 2011, a filming start date had not been set, the movie's described as a cross between *Taken* and *Die Hard*.

In the movie, Taylor plays a college student on spring break in Cancun, Mexico. He and his friends are

kidnapped and held hostage by bad guys. It is up to Taylor's character (and martial arts training) to save them.

Fans also looked forward to seeing lots more of Taylor in 2011. *Breaking Dawn—Part 1*—the first half of the movie based on the fourth *Twilight* book—was set to open November 18, 2011. In 2011, Taylor also stars in a thriller called *Abduction*. Taylor plays Nathan, a young man shocked to find his own baby photo on a missing persons Web site. The story follows his search for the truth.

The year 2012 will be another busy year for Taylor. According to The Internet Movie Database, *Breaking Dawn—Part 2* comes out on November 16, 2012. Taylor will be heavily involved in promoting that film.

Entertainment publications say that in 2013, Taylor will star in two films. In *Incarceron*, Taylor is cast as the lead character, Finn, and *Harry Potter*'s Emma Watson depicts his love interest, Claudia. He also stars as Stretch in the 3-D action movie *Stretch Armstrong*. The film is based on a flexible action figure that was popular in the 1970s.

Some young actors fade away as they get older. Taylor Lautner is one star that will continue to shine for years to come. He has many big films in the works that are sure to dazzle his fans.

Timeline

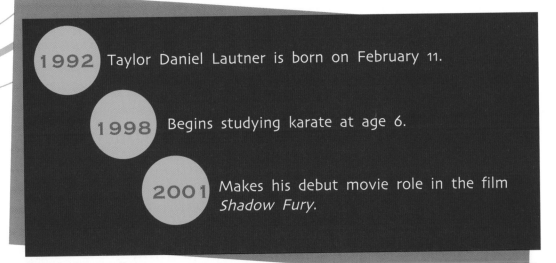

1992 Taylor Daniel Lautner is born on February 11.

1998 Begins studying karate at age 6.

2001 Makes his debut movie role in the film *Shadow Fury*.

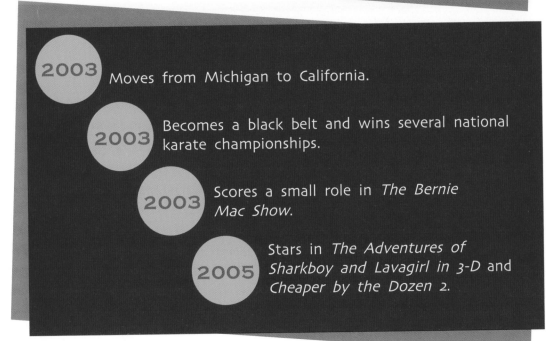

2003 Moves from Michigan to California.

2003 Becomes a black belt and wins several national karate championships.

2003 Scores a small role in *The Bernie Mac Show*.

2005 Stars in *The Adventures of Sharkboy and Lavagirl in 3-D* and *Cheaper by the Dozen 2*.

2008 Lands the part of Jacob Black in *Twilight*.

2009 Taylor's dad forms his own production company, Tailor Made Entertainment.

2009 *The Twilight Saga: New Moon* hits movie theaters.

2010 Appears in the movie *Valentine's Day* with Taylor Swift and *The Twilight Saga: Eclipse*.

2010 Wins People's Choice award for Favorite Breakout Movie Actor in January, wins Nickelodeon's 2010 Kids' Choice award for The Best Movie Actor in March, and wins Choice Hottie at 2010 Teen Choice Awards in August.

2011 Nominated for People's Choice Award for Best Movie Actor; Won People's Choice Award for Best On-Screen Team (with Kristin Stewart and Robert Pattinson).

Further Info

Books

Carpenter, Amy. *The Taylor Lautner Album*. Medford, NJ: Plexus Publishing, Inc., 2009.

Ryals, Lexi. *Taylor Lautner: An Unauthorized Biography* (Get the Scoop). New York: Price Stern Sloan, 2009.

Williams, Mel. *Taylor Lautner: Overnight Sizzlin' Sensation*. New York: Simon Pulse, 2009.

Internet Addresses

The Internet Movie Database: Taylor Lautner
http://www.imdb.com/name/nm1210124/

Official Web site of Stephenie Meyer
http://www.stepheniemeyer.com/

Taylor Lautner, a Fan Site
http://taylor-lautner.com/

Complete Filmography

2001: *Shadow Fury*, Young Kismet

2005: *Cheaper by the Dozen 2*, Eliot Murtaugh

2005: *The Adventures of Sharkboy and Lavagirl in 3-D*, Sharkboy

2008: *Twilight*, Jacob Black

2009: *The Twilight Saga: New Moon*, Jacob Black

2010: *Valentine's Day*, Willy Harrington

2010: *The Twilight Saga: Eclipse*, Jacob Black

2011: *Abduction*, Nathan

2011: *The Twilight Saga—Breaking Dawn—Part 1*, Jacob Black

2012: *The Twilight Saga: Breaking Dawn—Part 2*, Jacob Black

2013: *Stretch Armstrong*, Stretch Armstrong

2013: *Incarceron*, Finn

Glossary

auction—A publicly held sale at which property or goods are sold to the highest bidder.

audition—A tryout for an actor or singer.

callback—A request for a performer to audition again.

encouraged—Urged or inspired.

karate—A self-defense method that does not use weapons.

martial arts—Traditional forms of self-defense or combat that use punches, kicks, and throws.

overachiever—One who performs better than expected on the basis of his or her age or talents.

paparazzi—Photographers who take candid celebrity photos.

Quileute—American Indian people found in Washington.

red-eye—An airline flight that departs very late at night.

vigorously—Energetically, forcefully and powerfully.

Index